FROM
ANGER
TO
ACTION

20 Poems

By John C. Lardner/Devdatt

Published by Integrative Equivalence Publications, 2019
7 Robertson Place, Forres, Scotland, IV36 1EU

Copyright: John C. Lardner©2019

ISBN: 978-1-5272-3830-5

The moral right of the author has been asserted

Printed in Scotland by: Big Sky Print Ltd., The Press Building, 305 The Park, Findhorn, Forres, Scotland, IV363TE

Dedication

To Greta Thunberg,
the world's young people,
members of *Extinction Rebellion*,
and all who agree that the time to
save our planet is well over due.

'We have to understand the emergency of the situation. Our leadership has failed us. Young people must hold older generations accountable for the mess they have created. We need to get angry, and transform that anger into action.'

Greta Thunberg, 16, *Twitter post,* 23 December 2018

Contents

Introduction

Poems

Poem 1:	The Butterfly
Poem 2:	Bedroom Tax
Poem 3:	Greed is Good
Poem 4:	Angry
Poem 5:	Elephants
Poem 6:	The Postie
Poem 7:	Hold Me Close
Poem 8:	Stone and I
Poem 9:	Water
Poem 10:	Happy Christmas
Poem 11:	Drumbeats
Poem 12:	The Last Man
Poem 13:	Twin Towers
Poem 14:	Blue Planet Rap
Poem 15:	Digital Jam
Poem 16:	Three Tweets for the Times
Poem 17:	Glowing Away
Poem 18:	Survival of the Fittest
Poem 19:	Golden Goose
Poem 20:	The Last Poem To My Children & Grandchildren (Composed by the reader?)

Conclusion

Addendum

Acknowledgements

'Because we cannot save ourselves without contesting oligarchic control, the fight for democracy and justice and the fight against environmental breakdown are one and the same. Do not allow those who have caused this crisis to define the limits of political action. Do not allow those whose magical thinking got us into this mess to tell us what can and cannot be done'

George Monbiot,
'The Earth is in a Death Spiral: The Only Hope is Radical Action',
The Guardian, Wednesday 14 November 2018

'Hannah Arendt, referring to her work on the origins of totalitarianism [or in this case 'oligarchic control' and 'environmental breakdown'][1] wrote that "the natural human reaction to such conditions is one of anger and indignation because these conditions are against the dignity of man. If I describe these conditions without permitting my indignation to interfere, then I have lifted this particular phenomenon out of its context in human society and have thereby robbed it of part of its nature, deprived it of one of its important inherent qualities."'

Shoshana Zuboff,
The Age of Surveillance Capitalism:
The Fight for a Human Future at the New Frontier of Power
(Profile Books: London), 2019, 522

---

[1] See Hannah Arendt, "A Reply" [to Eric Voegelin's review of Hannah Arendt, *The Origins of Totalitarianism*], in *Review of Politics*, 15 (1953): 79.

Introduction

'It is worse, much worse, than you think.' (3)
David Wallace-Wells.
The Uninhabitable Earth: A Story of the Future
(Allen Lane/Penguin), 2019

'Our house is on fire. I am here to say, our house is on fire. [...] I want you to act as you would in a crisis. I want you to act as if our house is on fire; because it is.'
Greta Thunberg, 16, talking about climate change at the
World Economic Forum 2019

Introduction

I'm angry, so angry that I wrote a poem called 'Angry' (**Poem 4**, below) this is the 1st verse:
I am angry, yes I am
Angry at the ignorance of man,
Angry at such gross disease
That leaves us all so ill at ease;
Angry at this waste and cost,
The despoliation, the irreparable loss
Of nature's gifts and bounteous store,
All because we just want more,
And more and more and even more;
Who can ever keep the score?

....and someone then described me as 'the Angry Poet'. However, I'm not the only one who is angry, if I were the only one we would not have Donald Trump or BREXIT or the rise of Fascism in Hungary, Italy, Brazil, and elsewhere. This anger has two causes I think – both related:

1) The unequal Social and Economic System we are living within.
2) The Environmental Crisis and Climate change we are now experiencing and clearly witnessing.

Both were brought into stark relief recently by articles in *The Observer* and *The Guardian*: the first is an article about *Surveillance Capitalism*. *Surveillance Capitalism* aims to manipulate our survival needs by surreptitiously controlling the environment and context in which we live *via* the data they collect about us, in order to extract money and profit. As the bye-line went: 'it is no longer enough to automate information flows about us: the goal is to automate us.' Thus man's nature is undermined for profit. [2]

---

[2] See John Naughton, 'The New Capitalism' on Shoshana Zuboff's new book, *The Age of Surveillance Capitalism*, in *The Observer: The New Review*, 20 January 2019, 16-21. Thus Zuboff interviewed by Naughton makes the following point: 'It is no longer enough to automate information flows about us: the goal is now to automate us. These processes are meticulously designed to produce ignorance by circumventing individual awareness and thus eliminate any possibility of self-determination. As one data scientist explained, "We can engineer the context around a particular behaviour and force change that

Then I read a second article which emphasised that:

'When the fruits of change have fallen on the US [and obviously too the UK] in recent decades the very fortunate have basketed almost all of them; for instance the average pre-tax income of the top tenth of Americans has doubled since 1980, that of the top 1% has tripled, and that of the top 0.001% has risen sevenfold. [3]

Further down the system 'the fruits of change' have stagnated or gone into reverse. Thus is man's enjoyment of a full Life reduced to an increasingly unequal struggle to simply survive; under such a machine-orientated system is it any wonder that our natural environment and so our pressing Climate Emergency is not being fully addressed?

Thus, I come to my third article, 'Alarm over sea level as Greenland ice melt accelerates'. Thus Oliver Milman writes:

'The research provides fresh evidence of the dangers posed to vulnerable coastal places as diverse as Miami, Bangladesh and various Pacific Islands as climate change shrinks the world's land-based ice.
"The only thing we can do is adapt and mitigate further global warming – it is too late for there to be no effect," [Michael] Bevis [Professor of Geodynamics at Ohio State Univ.] said. "This is going to cause additional sea level rise. We are watching the ice sheet hit a tipping point. We're going to see faster and faster sea level rise for the foreseeable future. Once you hit that tipping point the only question is how severe does it get?' [4]

This is February 2019, we have known about Global Warming and its dangers since at least 1990, and yet despite the efforts of environmentalists

---

way...We are learning how to write the music, and then we let the music make them dance."' See also page 33 (note 7) and the Addendum on page 61 (note 10).
[3] Anand Giridharadas 'The new elite's phoney crusade to save the world', *The Guardian*, Tues. 22 January 2019, 'Journal', 9; Also see, Anand Giridharadas, *Winners Take All: The Elite Charade of Changing the World* (Allen Lane), 2018/19.
[4] Oliver Milman, 'Alarm over sea level as Greenland ice melt accelerates', *The Guardian*, Tues. 22 January 2019, 1 & 4.

and others the situation has worsened 'The System' ploughs on regardless – there is too much wealth and profit to be garnered for the 'fortunate few'.

Of course it is vital that each of us does what we can to change things, it is important that small and worthy projects are pursued but unless the overall context is conducive, unless the direction of development is changed in supportive ways, then the present unsustainable trajectory of constant growth will continue with severe existential and civilisational consequences, or even civilisational collapse, as David Attenborough pointed out in Poland (December 2018) and reiterated at Davos (January 2019).

This is where spiritual activism must-needs become much more assertive if catastrophe is to be averted. We need perhaps more than hope, warm words, and worthy projects, we need to move from anger (with all its associated feelings of fear, sadness, grief, pain) to action (which of course does not rule out all these other feelings). The vote was only won for men and women via assertive action (think not only of the suffragists but also the suffragettes). Workers rights were not achieved by simply hoping for the best, but by concrete actions. Saving our world is not a political decision, even though many would try to pigeonhole it as one and so dismiss it – it is a moral and spiritual decision. We do it because we must – without thought of whether we will succeed or not – we do it because it is the right thing to do; and not only for us but for our children, our grandchildren and for the next seven generations.

There is a fuzzy boundary between the political and the moral but like all seekers of change it is a challenge: if we hold back from challenging the *status quo* then maybe our children and grandchildren (and we ourselves) will blame us for a lack of courage and leadership, but it is also challenging because it makes us outsiders of the mainstream society of which we are also a part, and in which many of us, most of us have a stake and so fear losing. The needs of Life as a Whole are so often confounded by the needs of survival and comfort.

It seems to me we must address this crisis of climate change as a matter of urgency. For too long it has been badly neglected by mainstream politicians and the media. Nonetheless it has inevitably been lurking in the background, in the questions, in the fears, practical aims and aspirations, especially of the younger generation who might ask, after all these years why has so little changed? And how can we move from this apparent complacency to a much more dynamic and pro-active position – one even open to direct action, civil disobedience and peaceful protest.

In the 1930s Gandhi was a rebel, and led the Indian Independence rebellion. He was rebelling, peacefully against Britain for independence; the *Extinction Rebellion* is even more vital for it is about rebelling against the very real possibility, indeed probability that much of the living world, and indeed humanity may cease to be able to exist in the future.

As Linda Hogan puts it

'It is, perhaps, the darkest pain of the contemporary human that we are losing everything of true worth from this world [i.e. all that speaks of Life in all its intrinsic fullness]. In all the four directions, the animals are leaving. Through our failed humanity they are vanishing.' [5]

All because of erroneous and mistaken ideas of economic growth and development it seems that 'The Animals are Leaving', which ultimately includes us; it seems to me such a rebellion, indeed an *Extinction Rebellion*, is, under the circumstances, only right and proper.

---

[5] See Linda Hogan, quoted by Nick Totton, *Wild Therapy: Undomesticating Inner and Outer Worlds* (PCCS Books: Monmouth), 2017, 204; from, Linda Hogan, 'First people'. In Linda Hogan, D. Metzger & B. Peterson, eds., *Intimate Nature: The bond between women and animals* (Fawcett Columbine: New York), 1998, 6-19.

The Poems

'The threat from climate change is more total than from the bomb. It is also more pervasive. In a 2018 paper, forty two scientists [6] from around the world warned that, in a business-as-usual scenario, no ecosystem on earth is safe, with transformation "ubiquitous and dramatic," exceeding in just one or two centuries the amount of change that unfolded in the most dramatic periods of transformation in the earth's history over tens of thousands of years.' (226)

David Wallace-Wells.
The Uninhabitable Earth: A Story of the Future
(Allen Lane/Penguin), 2019

---

[6] See Connor Nolan et al., "Past and Future Global Transformation of Terrestrial Ecosystems Under Climate Change," *Science* 361, no. 6405 (August 2018): 920-23.

Poem 1:
The Butterfly
(John C. Lardner – Sunday 5th April 2015)

1
I fly, I am a butter-fly,
In the day enjoying the warm sunshine.
I have emerged from my chrysalis.
I am transformed into the light,
I am the light, the sun, as
I am the butterfly – free at last.

2
I live in love and light.
I live life and love, in the warm sunshine.
I am born again, though I may
Appear to have descended into chaos,
But this is the chaos of freedom,
The very opposite of ordered bondage.

3
Why be a moth immolating itself
On the bright flame of another's sun,
When I may be the butterfly
Caressed by the breeze and warmth
That takes us all forward
That gives life and love to all?

4
I am the butterfly, the breeze,
And the sun, as I am the moth
That seeks self-immolation under the moon.
I breathe life into all, I am all,
Both sun and moon, butterfly and moth.

5
Am I one who needs another?

I am One! Who needs another?

And yet:

6
I AM one who needs another
To contain and channel me
To keep my wholeness whole
And in me, through all contradictions,
Through all opposites and paradoxes.

7
I AM one who needs another,
To learn the ambivalence
Of polarised voices, of point
And counter-point, hope and despair,
Of sadness and anger, holding and letting go.

8
Only then can I become
That One that may know
I am One! And may ask,
Playfully, who needs another?

Poem 2:
Bedroom Tax
(John C. Lardner – 23rd June 2013, modified 26/27th April 2014)

1
'Put the family first,' they said,
'Keep our families let them thrive,
This is what we want,' they cried;
But in truth it's a false display,
Where should Gran go,
When she comes to stay?
What of brothers, John and Jim?
Of sister Ann and cousin Fin?

2
Many families by divorce divided
Need bed and board to be reconciled.
How can our families now survive,
Let alone go forth and thrive,
When the found, the very base,
Of hearth and home,
Are all but erased......
When loved ones begin another phase.

3
And what if fortune does not smile
On John or Jim, Ann or Fin?
Where's the home, they can return to
When life's dreams are left in turmoil?
For their bedrooms, once vacated,
Are now taxed
As space that's wasted....
Such is the state with which we're fated.

4
Sadly it's the blatant truth,
Such government's not for me or you,
The ordinary run of men and women
Struggling in a world so unforgiving.
And truth be said they like it so
Keep them poor, weak and anxious
Where all resistance
Is met with sanctions.

5
Keep all divided one on one
So all resistance is undone;
Let the poor keep their own
We dare not tolerate a stable home.
For such as they, it's just not fair
That some should have a place to be
While others shirk,
Though no work there be.

6
Even if we talk of moving,
To cut the tax of which
They're so approving,
There are no smaller homes to go to
Yet empty houses stand row on row.
Meanwhile the poor and disabled
Live distressed and are de-stabled.
Fairness? No! Please change the label.

7
And so it seems we've missed the bus
In a land we once could trust.
Where all could stand and be together,
One nation proud, one all together.
But it seems the rich and wealthy
Become both proud and condemnatory.
While they enjoy their greedy bonus
We are betrayed, our hope's erroneous.

8
'tis Thatcher's children – harsh and steely –
Who will come to rue the day they freely
Imposed this bedroom tax, we call it,
A return to a Poor Law audit.
What was once the 'workhouse test'
Is now a surplus 'bedroom test;' there is no rest
If you are sick and broke.
A castle-home? It's a cruel joke!

9
Workhouse, poll tax, means test, more?
It's pain and sorrow if you're poor.
A rich man in his mansion fine
May have many bedrooms, 'just divine.'
But where a wheel chair person rides,
It's undeserved riches the bonus banker spies.
"Why should this cripple have a carer standing,
In a bedroom, on a nearby landing?"

10
Thus we live an in-cohesive state;
"There's no justice for you, mate!"
Let's turn men and women into jugglers
It's zero-hours that confront such strugglers.
'It's a fate of their own making,'
Meanwhile a hefty profit's waiting!
Is this the price we all must pay
To just survive from day to day?

11
This unequal land may not be lived in.
We will change it, it's our mission
To offer care, concern and play,
Where all can have a proper say,
A place to stay, and decent pay.

Poem 3:
Greed is Good
(John C. Lardner – 10th August 2013, modified May 2014)

1
In the '60s we were told
We must advance, we must
be bold.
In the white heat of technology
Is the place we need to be,
And for those who complained
and doubted:
'It's progress init?'
Their opponents shouted.

2
In the '80s we were told
We must advance, the dream's
run cold.
Not in making is the future,
But in banking, shares and futures,
And for those who complained
and doubted:
'Greed is good,'
Their opponents shouted

3
In the noughties we're now told
We must advance, all must
be sold.
In the global world it is survival
That demands economic revival,
And for those who complain
and doubt:
'Don't rock the boat,'
Their opponents shout.

4
Yet all along it seems to us to be
It's the complaining doubters
who truly see,
Who really felt their sums to do –
An instinctive creed beyond the school –
And will those who shout
us down
Repent the greed
In which all will drown?

Poem 4:
Angry
(John C. Lardner – 20th May 2014)

1
I am angry, yes I am,
Angry at the ignorance of man
Angry at such gross disease
That leaves us all so ill at ease;
Angry at this waste and cost,
The despoliation, the irreparable loss
Of nature's gifts and bounteous store,
All because we just want more,
And more and more and even more;
Who can ever keep the score?

2
With species lost, a land defiled,
Weather wrecked, protest reviled,
Must we stand so meek and mild
While yet more toxic trends are trialled?
And so it seems the eye is turned
Blinded by such good returns,
Enjoy the profit while nature burns,
...Sad such glory man so spurns.
Spell-bound by such glitzy wealth
Our inheritance is destroyed by stealth.

3
Shaving here and shaving there,
A mere 5% so we don't care!
Still a token's left to see
(But such a shrivelled entity);
Let's celebrate our victory
In the global race we'll yet be free.
But what's this freedom in the end
If it's to hell that we descend,
Down and down and further still
Bound to the very pit of hell?

4

If we can destroy by law
What's the point? Let's destroy more
In an orgy, out beyond, so
No cautious mind will dare respond.
But we ask what point the law
If no balance it can restore,
No sustaining moderation,
To restrain and bring salvation?
When the boundless outlaw rides
A silent justice mocks our cries.

5

Observing the politics of man
It's impossible to understand
How it is we make the laws,
Creating systems with such flaws.
If through man's justice and man's laws
Nature's balance we'll not restore
Then nature's law goes as before,
For nature is our greater law.
If we can't curtail demand
No endless supply may we command.

6

At some point in place and time,
A tipping point reveals the line,
A cavalcade of men, of women,
Pushed beyond the bounds of living,
Tearing down the 'rules of reason,'
Condemning such unnatural treason.
So smooth the logic of the pen
It does confound the wit of men
Until in wrath – with anger loaded:
'We were duped,' the mob exploded.

7

And so it is at some time's end
It's not on reasoned logic we'll depend
For as David Hume surmised
Do not our sentiments deride.
What will save us, if aught can,
Will be the clever heart of man.
It is the source – deep and rare –
The only counter to despair,
The only answer at which we stare.

8

So if our civilisation's lost
Burdened by unsustainable cost,
Brought down by selfishness and greed,
Bland denial, a mendacious creed,
It is because we've lost the will,
To stand, be counted, sure and still,
To wage jihad, the holy war,
To thwart the greedy creed of more.
Only sure and constant courage
Can outwit this growing outrage.

9

I am angry, yes I am,
Angry at the ignorance of man
Angry at such gross disease
That leaves us all so ill at ease;
Angry at this waste and cost,
The despoliation, the irreparable loss
Of nature's gifts and bounteous store,
All because we just want more,
And more and more and even more;
God's indifferent to the final score.

Poem 5:
Elephants
(John C. Lardner – 5th July 2014)

1

A flash, a bang, a roar, a crash,
A natural wonder bites the dust.
A bright red fountain, a darkening pool,
I see red, the hunter too.
I ask myself: "Who's the greater fool?
Is it I, who this horror beholds,
Or the hunter as his smile unfolds?"
Before us, lumpen, in death inert,
A dollarized ivory treasure trove
Protrudes beyond the mountainous flesh
Lying cast adrift upon the veldt.

2

Is this the price that must be paid
So others may be conserved, be saved,
A little longer, while we adjust
To the knowledge they will all be lost
Like so much else we love and trust?
Time and again we find a line
That seemed so clear and well defined,
Is yet crossed and much maligned
Because the human tide demands
Another income, house and land;
Non-human nature's needs be damned!

3
Despite the oaths so solemnly given,
To effect a policy decision,
No airport runway here they promised,
And yet it's we who are admonished,
For standing in the future's way.
Come what may, despite all we say,
It's the privatised state that wins the day.
In similar vein who'll stand to gain
When the green belt's finally breached
And planning rules go up in smoke
Was all this lost before we awoke?

4
The more it is we take and kill,
As we exploit with mechanised skill,
The more that is repressed-depressed.
It does not go away you know
But lies beneath in our deeper soul,
Gnawing at it piece by piece
So much that it destroys our sleep.
The 'other' that was safely 'there',
Leaving others in despair
Now comes home to haunt us still,
Our nightmares dark, our chatter shrill.

5
With each barren waste created,
Each pride of nature killed or crated,
The brain contorts, cavorts and spins,
As outer conquest comes, we lose, it wins.
As herds, so starved and hunted, die,
Their ghosts reborn within us thrive.
And as the elephantine silence grows
Its soundless secret truth we mow,
To keep our manicured lawns, 'just so.'
Cut to the quick to enforce denial
Our chaotic world of lies out spirals.

6
Elephants never forget they say
Though we may forget the time of day,
Or what it means to be in play;
Silent, standing within each room,
Unexplored, deplored, ignored, and grim.
In this sad depleted state,
I spy their brothers of lighter hue,
White elephants trumpeting a vanity trill,
Serving the vainglorious will
To distract the demented soul
As shod in red it whirls and swirls.

7
Where is the path that we must tread
To avoid the end we dread?
To survive from day to day
So we hasten what we dismay;
The trials, the trends, the deathly hallows
Extinguished nature, reduced, made shallow.
Yet to sustain the deeper whole
Demands we stand erect, say 'NO',
No more windfalls for the greedy few
No more contorted science of matter
Destroying all, and so our dreams to shatter.

8
And now I feel impelled to write
A final verse of inspiring, hopeful sight,
To offer friend and foe alike
A wholesome future, a civilised life.
And yet it is the truth for me,
That in all the chaos that I see,
The truth which saves (me) lies within.
The truth which forgives the sins of man
Within a Good and Godly soul,
That sees herewith a hypothetical world,
Which succeed or fail, *I* am yet whole.

Poem 6:
The Postie
(John C. Lardner – 15th August 2014)

1
Once upon a time I would greet the postie
With a smile and a hearty line
About the day, as our ways we'd wend.
This I did to affirm the man,
And his van, for all they did
To make our lives, and communities, complete.

2
Also in mind was the sense of
The venerable institution, represented
In the postie, and his van,
Standing behind us both,
A benevolent presence bringing us
Into the nation's ambit – one and free.

3
Now I still greet the postie
With a smile and a hearty line,
Because of the man he is.
However, the Royal Mail is now
A hollow form – an institution
Re-born for profit, its national purpose thwarted.

4
Thus it represents what our nation's become,
A flag, a badge, a superficial form
Masking the fragments of incoherence,
Where predators prowl on innocent kindness
Where to care is construed as
A mere grooming for future use.

Poem 7:
Hold Me Close
(John C. Lardner – Thursday 19th February 2015)

1
You hold me close, yet could not reach my soul.
You hold me close, yet would not read my words,
Those I wrote for you hoping to be heard;
When a robin sings I live,
When its nest falls, when the nestling tree
Is thoughtlessly carelessly and unnecessarily felled,
I die.

2
And death comes like a winter freeze,
The stabbing thrust of frost, that sharp breath-take
The realisation, sudden, shattering and
Wide-eyed, I am alone.
A world has ended, life's tree felled,
Thoughtlessly, carelessly and unnecessarily felled,
We die.

3
We live in an ever more boundaried world.
The definitions tighten, the facts sharpen,
The concepts, ever clearer, mark the edge,
Hardened like stone.
The gentle trees defining nature's edge are felled,
Thoughtlessly, carelessly and unnecessarily felled,
Robin dies.

Poem 8:
Stone and I
(John C. Lardner – Thursday 19th February 2015)

1
And the great mythologist, Joseph Campbell,
Whose ideas gave structure to *Star Wars*,
Said great stories are of one basic form:
The hero goes forth, is initiated and returns.
My stone and I share this story.
In our case neither is complete.
We have both gone forth,
But initiation and return
Are still in question.

2
Stone sallied forth in fluidity and movement,
A story crystallised in veined and mottled hints,
Evidence of what lies within,
Now apparently set in stone for ever more.
I sallied forth in fluidity and movement,
The pregnant substance of conception,
The bloodied emergence of my birth,
And from child to man in world's embrace – stone
And I suspended in the moment.

3
What initiation does this now draw on?
Stone's timescale stretches far behind
And beyond mine – in all probability,
Unless crushed for road-stone or other use.
Am I too to be crushed by a stony load,
Too petrified to move and breath life's fresh air?
Stone lies apparently inert indifferently at one
With all that lies within and beyond
Its veined and mottled surface form.

4

I lie, or stand, or sit, carrying my
Appearance as I go. Initiation will come,
I like stone must be cooked in the furnace,
Know that ever present moment
In the flicker of my birth and death.
So short the coming and going of flesh
Compared to the ebb and flow of the stony earth;
Yet our cycles interleave at every moment;
Such being is 'to be' initiated.

5

Thence the long, or short return,
Two sub-plots, within their universal play,
Are stone and I. Surely the initiation
Is to know we are both, indeed, all
One, and once Known, then return.
How stone knows this I know not,
But to know not is to Know God.
To Know this I am both God-fearing and atheist,
So stone, solidly indifferent is both God and not.

Poem 9:
Water
(John C. Lardner – Thursday 26th February 2015)

1
Truth, like water, ripples through
The world in timeless flow –
It is simply there.

2
It asks for nothing, yet buoys us up,
And yet acts as a liquid glass –
A mirror to the soul.

3
Truth, like water, has nothing to hide,
Yet what monsters lurk
within its murky depth?

Poem 10:
Happy Christmas
(John C. Lardner – Tuesday 22nd November 2016)

1
Happy Christmas one and all,
To the bonus banker and CEO
Whose pay is bought upon the backs
Of 'efficiency savings' from the lower ranks.

2
Happy Christmas to the poor
Who dare to ask, can we have more
For warmth and shelter from the storm
And that food enough might be the norm?

3
Happy Christmas to the stony hearts,
The Gradgrinds of a returning past,
Who only value data sheets
And not the misery meted out
To zero workers with no clout, to shout about.

4
Happy Christmas to those who have
Decided it must be this way
(IT NEEDN'T)
For all we have we deserve they say.
It is not us who cause you pain
It's market forces that are to blame.
And who are governments to interfere
So that Christmas might be less austere?

5
Let Happy Christmas warm the heart,
Let the coming year make a start,
So all may share the nation's bounty,
The length and breadth of every shire and county
Of our once great, now sad, diminished country.

Poem 11:
Drumbeats
(John C. Lardner – 3rd May 2017)

1
The drumbeats of war
Tock-tick the countdown
To our barbarian night.

2
As we 'machine tickling
aphids' march blindly;
As constitutions crumble. [7]

3
We drown in a grey goo
Of boundless possibilities and
Of deeply denied despair.

4
We kill the God outwith
And within, so who
Can we ask to save us?

5
Man's destructive creativity
Smacks of a certain
Arrogance of youth.

6
Hubris sings the siren
Song, and down we go
Into dark's endless night.

---

[7] 'Samuel Butler predicted in *Erewhon*, published in 1872, that we might become "machine-tickling aphids" – parasites upon machines. This novel [*Sympathy* by Olivia Sudjic] convincingly updates and extends the idea that what we think we are using [i.e. machines/automation] may, in fact, be using us. Shudder – and then post about it. The abyss beckons' (See Hermione Eyre, 'A sharp story of obsession and technology, this up-to-the-minute debut explores what smart phones are doing to our souls' in Review, 10, *The Guardian*, Saturday 27th May 2017); see also page 8 (note 2) and page 61 (note 10).

Poem 12:

The Last Man

(John C. Lardner – Friday 2nd June 2017)

– I –

1
The last man; and it was a man, stood alone, all one, but lonely, for he was the last one, the last of humanity – almost the last living entity on earth. From his mountain-top eerie, within his protective bubble of artificiality he looked out and surveyed the bleak devastated landscape below him.

2
It was hot outside, very hot and very dry – global warming had won out over all counter-veiling measures. Inside, however, behind the transparent shield it was cool and comfortable – at least for now. Yet he found this comfort excruciating for it was false, unnatural, machine-dependent.

3
Banks of machines and automated devices measured and monitored his vital physical-survival needs so that he might remain within an optimum range of comfort. But was he really comfortable? Indeed so comfortable was he that he wanted to scream silently to escape this hell on earth.

– II –

4
He was the richest man in the world, or had been up until the time it ceased to matter. His youth had been comfortable – idyllic: the product of a seemingly close middle-class family whose comfort had been bought upon the backs of workers earning 100s, from which they made 1000s.

5
They were secure behind a high walled house and garden – substantial, lush green, bright flowers, tall trees. This was not by chance but the product of hard work, decent and respectable endeavour. In this competitive world you had to look out for yourself against workers and colleagues.

6
This competition had a name – Darwinism: 'the survival of the fittest.' They survived because they were the fittest and so deserved to survive and live well. Another name for it was capitalism – the free market, the 'invisible hand' and the 'animal spirits'. Thus each naturally found their place.

7
Yet the stark reality of competition and survival was masked from view, certain constraints seemed to soften the harshness: the strange idea of a loving God; that despite a 'dog eat dog world' one 'red in tooth and claw' yet there was a natural justice, a notion of responsible common decency.

8
It was impolite and ill-mannered to dwell on the harsh realities of the world outside the garden. The patriarch-father, while he might see fit to beat his son, chastise his wife and daughter and patronise his workforce, yet was obviously an honourable man whose word was his bond unto death.

9
But times changed. The Church declined, God died, natural justice became obedience to laws (no matter how derived, or in whose interest), reason and decency became subject to the logic of immediate need satisfaction and efficiency, democratic restraint gave way to capitalistic indulgence.

– III –

10
Greed became good, the rest died along with God. At business school he learnt the art of creative accounting, and of making a stock market killing, and the rich pickings to be had from controlling a public good – housing or water – and milking it, extracting value, efficiently maximising profitability.

11
The last man got rich. His wealth left the old patriarch-father sunning himself in the gentle shade of his quaint old-fashioned house and garden. Mammon was the new God, he became addicted to porn – the porn of love-addiction, money and power; the more he got the more he craved.

12
It's said: "Cortez told the Aztec King Montezuma, that he had a disease that only gold could cure." History shows that the so-called cure only inflames the disease. For the last man the more he got the more he needed to feel safe and secure. The more predatory he became the more he feared others.

13
The poor and impoverished might seek revenge and retribution. The more he predated the more his peers and betters (those even richer than he) would prey on him. For safety's sake he and his predatory friends retreated into to a high-walled, well-gated, barb-wired 'communal protected' space.

14
This kept out the little people – those too poor and sad to escape paying tax – those he now despised as pathetic, beneath him and barely human. He travelled from fortified, beautified compound to fortified bright efficient compound ignorant of the 99% of the population he keenly exploited.

15
But the gated community did not protect him from jealous neighbours, nor neighbours from his jealousy – might some enjoy more wealth than he? He feared them and despite the apparently friendly joshing and seeming shows of goodwill yet each would beggar their neighbour if they could.

– IV –

16
As the world beyond his narrow, well-gated community became more challenging so greater was the protection needed to keep that 'other' world out. As unrestrained capital, exploited all human and natural resources to exhaustion so human hostility increased, and nature fought back.

17
Pollution pushed at the gates: the land fragmented and fractured; water resources were contaminated; topsoil erosion created food shortages and famine; oceans died and forests were felled for one-off gains. As his plastic, synthetic safety, and longevity increased, yet outside the world was dying.

18
As the world died, the more he sought safety from that death. One by one, astute business opportunities allowed him to buy-out his neighbours. Through luck and guile he became the richest man in his street, in his town and city, and indeed the richest man in his country and finally all the world.

19
As the world's richest man he could make himself the safest and securest man in the world. He purchased a great mountain in a dirt poor country, desperate for cash; indeed he might as well be buying the whole country – the last paradise on earth – a real bargain: He was a God atop a mountain.

20
He spent millions, billions and trillions on his place of protection; wealth siphoned off from impoverished neighbours, the poor and dispossessed; and resources unsustainably extracted from everywhere else – a fortress monitored by computers, serviced by machines, and patrolled by robots.

21
Among the lesser mountain top retreats of billionaire and trillionaire neighbours his was the most awesome and shocking. In the depleted lands between, the capitalist economy was imploding. Investment opportunities became ever riskier; bubbles burst, bankrupting and laying waste lives.

22
As the situation deteriorated, bankruptcies increased exponentially, and an, ever-more wealthy elite dominated everything. Millionaires went bankrupt and sold out to billionaires; they in turn succumbed to trillionaires. Power resided less and less in money, and more and more in material assets.

23
Mightiness became the stark measure of rightness, justice and the law were exposed for the charlatans that they were. On went the concentration of 'might' and power…and increasing levels of mistrust and betrayal in the survival wars. The richest man trusted no-one but his machines.

– VI –

24
Into the world rode the Four Horsemen of the Apocalypse – death, disease, starvation, war – and slew all before them. The once-upon-a-time Garden of Eden, the beautiful blue planet, was now a wasteland. And still death stalked the land: time to lock down, shut-down and be hermetically sealed.

25
Desperate stragglers found no succour at his gate, while he found no succour behind it! At least at the end the outsiders found some solace in each other's arms – even his home crew had deserted him preferring to embrace death than suffer his cold, mechanical, synthetic, inhumanity.

26
Only at the end did the millionaires realise that the 'system' had killed them, and the workers earlier. But still the billionaires and the trillionaires had hung on: "Yes," they said "we know, but we can't escape the system. The great capitalist machine – nature's way: survival of the fittest."

– VII –

27
Silent birds chirped silent laughter; Innumerable, recent and long extinct species smirked behind their veils of death, the great oceans bellowed their mockery at such unnatural naturalness of thought and belief. But it was too late; yet still the trillionaires thought they were immune, special.

28
Surely they thought their trillions would save them. But they weren't special, they weren't God's chosen – and there were no space-ship lifeboats to far planets. Finally fear and mutual mistrust killed all survivors of the earlier mega-deaths of billions. Trust machines? Machines eat men!

29
Now the richest man in the world stood alone. He was 'the system,' fully integrated, one with the machines, with the automated devices, robots and computers which plugged into him, or *vice versa*? He was Comforted and made comfortable by them – a man, made lean, mean and robotic.

30
Yet though inseparable from the automated system he remained 'other,' he was still a self. How-ever he tried, he knew being one did not make him safe and not separate for he was separate – a two. Automated mechanisms meant to secure him, left him ever more anxious, fearful, even terrified.

– VIII –

31
His separate self knew it was time to go, time to switch off the machines, finally turn the lights out so to speak, say "good night" to this dead world! But would they let him? The machines, devices, robots and computers were all programmed to secure his survival at all costs, it was their *raison d'être*.

32
If his survival depended on them, their continuance depended on him he was the last man – his life was all that mattered. They could never let – the one time richest man in the world – the last man cease, especially now that all other life had been extinguished. His computer said he must never die.

33
He must, he'd be forced to, live alone, lonely on this death-of a-living-hell-on-earth, forever. As he scanned his memory banks for associations with the words 'last' and 'lost' he knew he was 'The Last the of the Mohicans' – the last of his tribe, lost, alone – but now the last of his species.

34
He scanned further for 'lost' and 'last' he was now the last, the 'The Last of the Great Whales' lost on the ocean, now alone waiting to die, but no harpoon gun would save him from his fate worse than death. Sad Mohicans and bloodied whales became entrapped in strange loops of consciousness...

35

....playing forever, lasting forever into the eons of black space, on and on into eternity. That was it. He would now be forever the last of the last....lost in space.

Poem 13:
Twin Towers
(John C. Lardner – Saturday 17th June 2017)

1
It is the wrench which kills.
The shock and awe of twin towers blazing,
The loss of place – of play-place-space – as our
Home-beings become enclosed
And we are cleared away, the detritus of
An unwanted, unsought war against
The Self, to suit utilitarian ends.

2
Man's power-purpose of survival,
The search of the dispossessed for refuge,
Fuels our greed and our need to feel
The lust that brings cathartic relief,
Easing for a time the pain of denial;
Of our ignorance of Life's fullness and
Its immeasurable, complex, singularity.

3
Addiction fills the void, things become
The fetish that create false god-goals
As all is commodified, market driven,
Reduced to that which is saleable,
An objective freedom, a false liberty-taking,
With that, which may not really be
Bought short or brutally sold.

4
We make war on each other, make war
On the warm nurturing mother and,
On ourselves (though we are all One).
We split, cut up, divide and rule, and
Dissect with digital precision the reality
Of existence that is necessarily and
Essentially a single glorious Whole.

5
And what a price we pay to simply
Survive. We fight on and on and on
To see another new hope of a new day
Dawn-to-transform into another false
Dawn-to-delay, waylay, mislay
The way we need to take so we may
Annihilate our orgy of self-loathing.

6
So the control-obsessed sadist's born,
Revelling in power; dominance of
Mother, son, daughter, as they crawl,
Stumble, drown, fall. Freedom's right
To abuse, cheat – love reduced to power,
Freedom descending to choice –
How, what, when, where to exploit?

7
The masochist too is the split
Accompaniment to the cracked bell,
The hollowed out toll, tribute paid
To ensure a survival that imbues and
Infuses the inanimacy of things
With a shallow, surface ripple,
A placated plastic pastiche of life.

8
As the master-commander inflicts
Demands, so the commodified, fetishised
Victim etherealises that omnipotent
Dispenser of arbitrary relief – favours,
Crumbs from the master's table
That might, or might not, offer
Life or death, hope or despair.

9
"I hold the whip-hand," growled the
Master and commander as the
Branded, brothel-bonded bitches
Sashayed their charms before his
Brutish bovver-band of brothers
– Plastic performing pleasure dolls –
In his monstrous bling-gin palace.

10
And so the handmaids parrot their
Boundless patter of adoration. The
Plastic chorus chirping and chirruping
– birds tweeting, anticipating needs
Other than their own, as their own –
Imbuing cold, hard life-less-death
With their own subjugated vitality.

11
The libidinous intensity of omnipotence,
The libidinous intensity of impotence,
The tragic cleavage of the ruptured
Self-soul, the strategic cut of the
Detached, divided half-whole,
Descending the plughole's
Brain train dead
drain.

12

And thus the seemingly omnipotent,
Lacking life, are made impotent,
And the seemingly impotent – even
In their shallow omni-empathic
Desperation come, like the meek,
To inherit the earth. For the last
Shall be first, and the first last.

13

Sadist and masochist are two, as
They project their own dis-owned
Selves, one onto the other, each
Denying each their truth and validity.
But yet we can cleave to, just as we
Can cleave asunder, and own within,
That which formerly we denied.

14

I am 'This,' yes! But I am also *'That,'*
Recognising *'That'* which outwardly
I oppress; so too I see *'That'* I
But oppress myself. *'That'* which I
Judge in others is yet *'That'*
Judgement which is *'That'* judgement
of my Self I needs must own.

15

There is a joy in this recognition,
A eureka moment in this revelation.
Thus there is a rebirth – a new wholeness
A new life beyond disowned
Innocence, which is a denial of
The fullness of experience –
It is a re-flowering of possibility.

16
It is the promised-land, that flows,
With milk and honey, the New Jerusalem,
Not a never-never land
But an ever-present land,
An acceptance of the 'Paradox
Of the Self' Ah! The bliss and joy
Of holding this ambivalent Truth.

17
There, is the integrated core,
The irreducible Self – of Buddha's smile,
The benign blessing of The Christ,
Jesus, the Way of God, the Tao's Way,
To which Mohammed, Prophet
Of God, Allah, urged submission,
Enjoining peace, shanti, shalom.

18
It lies within, but acts outwith.
It appears mystical, magical, a mystery,
But is very practical, common-sensical,
(Not whimsical) but Worldly-wise.
It is the road to Life's completeness.
Beyond the limits of a life for survival.
We have a choice – Life or extinction!

19
Let us 'Trumpet' this Truth, loudly,
Clearly, so that we all 'May'
Hear the call. Is it hope or will
The sirens atop the Towers of Trump
Eclipse – drown out – the dark,
Danger-warning of 24 stories
Of a south London blackened shell.

20
Twin Towers, two worlds, define
Our future, hope-hopeless, black-
Blackened; bright-well-blinged,
Both empty. But united a fertile
Present may yet return. What was
Once wrenched out may yet
Re-ground, re-root, re-form.

21
The question is can we, will we? But surely too
We must be prepared to specifically ask:
"If not us, who? If not now when?"
For if not now....very soon...
Very, very, soon,
It will be....
NEVER!

Poem 14:
Blue Planet Rap
(John C. Lardner – Monday 1ˢᵗ January 2018)

1
Blue Planet 1,
Blue Planet too,
Planet Brown dead.
It's blood red –
Bled – though blind
Are the powers-that-be.

2
Dread end, dead end,
Blue, blue sea.
Can't they see
Bound to the dosh,
Under the cosh,
Stashing the cash…

3
…Dreading to be free.
I want out.
It's not me,
Living for the time
When all'll be free.

4
Let's get mad,
Let's get bad,
No more sad,
Is what we'll be.

5
It must stop!
More than mad,
Worse than bad,
Sad, sad, sad.
I can't stand it,
Join with me.

6
End this mash up,
Throw this trash out.
They've had their turn,
See them squirm.

7
Question Time,
Question Trump,
Question May
Day by day.
Brexit Arm-a-geddon's
On its way.

8
Red stained sea,
Blue is me.
I would sue,
Would it help?
I think not,
Anni-hil-a-tion
Is what we've got.

Poem 15:
Digital Jam
(John C. Lardner – Wed. 22nd November 2017 to Tues 2nd January 2018)

1
We must act, you and I,
If the world is not to die,
For this, it will come to pass
All too soon – it will not last.

2
It can't sustain, the demands of man,
And the greed of those who can
Turn all the world, and all of man
'to digital dough,
Metaphysical jam...

3
...spread upon the empty waste,
A blood red jam, of bitter taste.
Drowning out the common weal
The little man, his hopes to steal.

4
Our government ministers
In Cabinet sit, with eyes agog
At the wealth of it.
The director's chair, executive lounge
The trade-off's clear,
They'll make no sound...

5
...Though their silence deafens!

Poem 16:
Three Tweets for the Times
(John C. Lardner – Tues 2nd January 2018)

                       Start

I Tweet to Trump
                  America First
                  America Last
                  America Lost

II Message to May
                  Heroic Brexit
                  Magic Brexit
                  Tragic Brexit

III Address to All
                  Arm-a-man
                  Arm-a-ment
                  Arm-a-geddon

                       Stop

                       The End

                Postscript! Encore!

IV Call to Complacency
                  Make-a-fortune
                  Gain-a-fortune
                  Mis-a-fortune

V Library Lament
                  Learning Libraries
                  Lending Libraries
                  Losing Libraries

VI Generation Greeting
                  Generation X
                  Generation Y
                  Generation Gone

                       Stop

                  The Final End

Poem 17:
Glowing Away
(John C. Lardner – Fri/Sat 9th/10th March 2018)

1
If the animals are leaving
Then so must I,
If Life is now departing
Then so, too I'm gone.

2
If the 'Silent Spring' is falling
Then I too will glow away,
If our wintry end is calling
Then it's clear I cannot stay.

3
If we are but mere machine
Then the die is all but cast,
As the system overwhelms me
Then too I must depart.

4
If the howling wolves are baying,
And baying for my blood,
Then I must go and join them
And trail where they have trod. [8]

---

[8] Fears of runaway climate change are real: 'Commenting on the findings [of Professor Johan Rockström's 'Hothouse Earth' Report] ...Dr Phil Williamson of the Univ. of East Anglia said, "In the context of the summer of 2018, this is definitely not a case of crying wolf, raising a false alarm.'
"The wolves are now in sight."
Kirsteen Paterson, '"Hothouse" Earth warning',
The National, Tuesday,
7 August, 2018, 10

Poem 18:
Survival of the Fittest
(John C. Lardner – Sunday 22nd July 2018)

1.
The 'survival of the fittest'
Will destroy the world –
Indeed is destroying it.

2.
The vitality of the healthy
Can heal the world –
If allowed to.

3.
But our time rapidly
Runs out –
Only God Knows.

Poem 19:
Golden Goose
(John C. Lardner – Thursday 8th November 2018)

1
It's greed will kill
The Golden Goose
The Golden Goose
The Golden Goose
Its greed will kill
The Golden Goose,
The goose that's almost gone.

2
And Gaia is
That Golden Goose
That Golden Goose
That Golden Goose
And Gaia is
That Golden Goose,
And Gaia's almost done.

3
It's man that kills
Our Great Green Globe
Our Great Green Globe
Our Great Green Globe
It's man that kills
Our Great Green Globe,
And all futures yet to come.

Poem 20:
The Last Poem
To My Children and Grandchildren
(Composed by the reader?)

Conclusion

'Personally, I think that climate change itself offers the most invigorating picture, in that even its cruelty flatters our sense of power, and in so doing calls the world, as one, to action.' (227-228)

David Wallace-Wells.
The Uninhabitable Earth: A Story of the Future
(Allen Lane/Penguin), 2019

Conclusion:
Letter to Douglas Ross
Member of Parliament for Moray

11th January 2019

Dear Douglas Ross M.P.,

May I wish you a Happy New Year and hope for better things in 2019. Please also find enclosed a booklet entitled From *Anger to Action: 20 Poems*. These include a number of poems I have written over recent years expressing my anger at what is happening to our world and our country. I have dedicated it to the activist group *Extinction Rebellion* because I am impressed by their commitment to holding the government to account in the light of climate change and the ecological emergency we face.

So serious is the problem that even David Attenborough expressed his fears for civilizational collapse recently at the climate change conference in Poland. Clearly much more serious and determined work needs to be done at once to limit global warming and environmental destruction. Back in the 1990s Margaret Thatcher expressed the view that climate change was the most dangerous threat facing the world. [9] It is very regrettable that her fears have not been met with more seriousness on the part of government.

Extinction Rebellion makes the point that responding promptly to the crisis is no longer a political choice but a moral imperative. Any government failing to protect its people from serious, especially existential danger loses the legitimate right to govern. It feels to me (and clearly many others) we are close to that point. Our country is in very serious political, social, economic and environmental trouble. 'Hostile environments' have been created in many areas and now we face the real danger of disorderly BREXIT.

---

[9] I would like to thank Douglas Ross for his prompt reply to this letter and his pointing out that Margaret Thatcher first raised the issue of climate change in 1988, for example in a speech to the *Royal Society* on Tuesday 27th September 1988. Even back then she noted how, 'the five warmest years in a century of records have all been in the 1980s.'

The main issue is the matter of 'trust'. Back in 2010 George Osborne promised in the wake of the Great Recession that 'we were all in this together' and then imposed a level of austerity that disproportionately damaged the poorest and most vulnerable members of our society. Austerity has been regularly criticised by religious leaders like the Archbishop of Canterbury, Justin Welby, international organisations such as the IMF, and of course most recently the UN Rapporteur on Poverty who described it as an ideological assault.

As George Monbiot's opening quote to my poems puts it the environmental crisis is inextricably bound up with our failing socio-economic system. Our democracy has been unable to hold capital to account for its destructive impact on both the manmade and natural environments. David Cameron announced, around the time George Osborne was declaring 'solidarity' that his would be 'the greenest government ever' but sadly the government record on the environment does not meet the needs of the moment. The government has:

1) *Scrapped support for onshore wind power*
2) *Removed subsidies for solar power*
3) *Ended the 'green homes' scheme*
4) *Sold off the Green Investment Bank*
5) *Given up on zero-carbon homes*
6) *Watered down the incentive to buy green cars*
7) *Abandoned the green tax target*
8) *Refused to support tidal power*
9) *Announced it will stop the solar panel feed in fee*
10) *Consistently supported 'fracking' in the teeth of widespread environmental and popular opposition.*

Of course at the root of the present crisis is our economic model which is wedded to unsustainable growth and development. Such levels of consumption can't continue on our finite planet if swathes of our natural environment let alone mankind as a species, and let alone our children and grandchildren, are to enjoy any future worth considering. This fundamental truth is largely ignored by the government, by the mainstream media and so the great majority of the population remain oblivious to the full dangers of the situation.

I would therefore urge you to listen carefully to what *Extinction Rebellion* is all about and (given that we are clearly facing an existential emergency similar to that of World War II) create a National Government embracing all shades of political opinion, including the full involvement of, and cooperation with, the devolved national governments of Scotland, Wales and Northern Ireland. To be successful it would demand the following. That:

1. The Government must tell the truth about the climate and wider ecological emergency, reverse inconsistent policies and work alongside the media to communicate with citizens.

2. The Government must enact legally binding policy measures to reduce carbon emissions to net zero by 2025 and to reduce consumption levels.

3. A national Citizen's Assembly to oversee the changes, as part of creating a democracy fit for purpose.

Extinction Rebellion is committed to an open and honest democracy and to the use of peaceful means and Non-Violent Direct Action in pursuit of these fully justified goals.

Yours most sincerely

John C. LARDNER
(cc to any interested parties)

Addendum

And finally the present threat to the *natural world*, that is the environmental crisis of climate change and ecological collapse (presaging 'civilisational collapse') is intimately related to a growing threat to our *human nature*. As Shoshana Zuboff points out: [10]

> *'For more than three centuries, industrial civilization aimed to exert control over nature for the sake of human betterment. Machines were our means of extending and overcoming the limits of the animal body so that we could accomplish this aim of domination. Only later did we begin to fathom the consequences: the Earth overwhelmed in peril as the delicate physical systems that once defined sea and sky gyrated out of control* [hence global warming, mass extinctions, etc.].
>
> *'Right now we are at the beginning of a new arc that I have called information civilization, and it repeats the same dangerous arrogance. The aim is not to dominate* **nature** *but rather* **human nature**. *The focus has shifted from machines that overcome the limits of bodies to machines that modify the behaviour of individuals, groups, and populations in the service of market objectives* [i.e. Surveillance Capitalism]. *This global installation of instrumentarian power overcomes and replaces the human inwardness that feeds the will to will and gives sustenance to our voices in the first person*[I as a subject]*, incapacitating democracy at its roots.'* (515)

Thus **nature** and our own **human nature** are both being undermined and threatened by extinction; this is due to the reduction of 'The Paradox of the Self' (that is Life) to the narrow logic of the machine and the algorithm, where all is either logical (supposedly always good), or contradictory (apparently always bad). While the former could be called monstrous thinking, the latter is perhaps magical thinking. However the Truth is almost certainly paradoxical and on this basis it is clear that an *Extinction Rebellion* is, more than ever, an absolutely moral and spiritual *natural right* – indeed it is a vital necessity. For too long all **nature** has been taken for granted and ruthlessly exploited: 'No more! Let this be our declaration.' (525)

---

[10] Shoshana Zuboff, *The Age of Surveillance Capitalism: The Fight for a Human Future at the New Frontier of Power* (Profile Books: London), 2019; also see page 8, and note 2 (above).

Acknowledgements

I acknowledge my parents, Brenda and Geoffrey, and my family and friends who, over the years have got me to this place; a life-point where I can give voice to all that concerns me closely: the future of our planet and the wondrous natural world to which it is home including our-selves; and the paradox of living, which is 'the paradox of the Self', which is the logic of Life.

Other friends from whom I derive support are the Quaker community, and the three choirs I sing with in Forres – the *Big Choir*, the *Sounds Deep* male choir, and the *Peace Songs* choir, as well as friends who are also *Friends of Findhorn Bay*, and others associated with the *Findhorn Foundation* and within the growing *Extinction Rebellion* movement that is taking shape.

It seems invidious to name names but specifically I would like to thank my piratical friend Dr Michael Williams and his specific belief in my 'voice', Lucy Fredman for affirming, deepening and extending the embodied vitality of my being; and more recently Laura Pasetti and her *Sacred Theatre* Group who have helped me channel my anger and self-knowledge towards intentional action and the meaning and purpose of poetry and drama.

I would wish to acknowledge my Guru, Swami Shyam, who died in 2017, who always lives within me, as does my dear sister, Vinamrita, and her partner, Nick, who remain at Swamiji's ashram in Kulu, H. P., India. Thank you too to Mick Drury and Pam Machin for their friendship and Pam for the photograph on the back cover of this book. My grateful appreciation to you all – named and unnamed – and, of course, to all in the non-human world.

Other specific pieces of material or influence that remain unacknowledged I apologise for and hope that the altruistic cause to which these poems are dedicated will induce forgiveness. I would emphasize too that the world we must move towards, if we are not only to survive but to really and fully 'Live', is one where enclosures, ownerships, and copyrights are less rigid than they are today and love, trust and long Life pervade the commonweal.

Finally I would wish to pay tribute to the extensive help of the library service of Moray – as ever under constant threat from the unnecessary 'cuts' due to the imposition of austerity following the *Great Recession* of 2007-2008.

'Why should I be studying for a future that soon may be no more, when no one is doing anything to save that future? And what is the point of learning facts when the most important facts clearly mean nothing to our society?'

'For 25 years, countless of people have stood in front of the United Nations Climate Change conference asking our nations' leaders to stop the emissions. But clearly this has not worked, since the emissions just continue to rise. So I will not ask them anything. Instead, I will ask the people around the world to realize that our political leaders have failed us, because we are facing an existential threat and there is no time to continue down this road of madness.'

Greta Thunberg;
Quoted in, "School Strike for Climate: Meet 15-year-old Activist Greta Thunberg, Who Inspired a Global Movement",
Democracy Now!, 11 December 2018.